Where in the World Will We Go Today?

Written by
Heather C. Toner
Illustrated by Bill Pazman

BQB
Alpharetta, Georgia

Where in the World Will We Go Today?
© 2014 Heather C. Toner. All rights reserved.

Published in the United States by BQB Publishing
(Boutique of Quality Books Publishing Company)
www.bqbpublishing.com

Printed in the United States of America

978-1-939371-546 (h)
978-1-939371-44-7 (p)
978-1-939371-45-4 (e)

Library of Congress Control Number: 2014939712

Book design by Meredith L. Burke, www.meredithburkedesigns.com

Dedication

For Keegan James—my inspiration . . . my world . . . my son.

Remember always son, that this world is your oyster. You can and will make it anything you desire.

There is nowhere you cannot go; there is nothing you cannot do.

Where in the world will we go today?

Where in the world will we stop and play?

2

Look around and you will see
How much fun this can be!

Where in the world will we go today?

Canada, Canada, what do you say?

Canada, Canada, we'll stop and play.

Toronto, Montreal, and Vancouver too.

Our friends from Canada are hoping you do . . .

See bear, elk, and wildlife galore.

The fishing is exceptional, the fun—even more!

Where in the world will we go today?

Portugal, Portugal, we'll stop and play.

Portugal, Portugal, a lively country.

Portugal, Portugal is where we'll be!

Portugal lies to the west of Spain,

Rising up by the ocean's mane.

Lisbon, the capital, is filled with glee!

Hear the songs of *fado* and happy you'll be!

7

Where in the world will we go today?

Peru, Peru, what do you say?

Peru, Peru, can you hear it calling you?

Peru, Peru, there is so much to do!
Lima, Machu Picchu, Galapagos too,
Nature abounds and is waiting for you!

Where in the world will we go today?

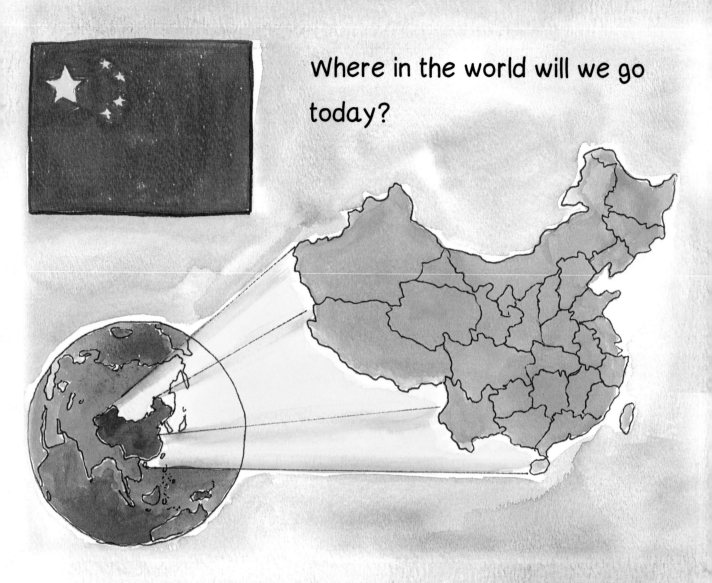

China, China, what do you say?

China, China, so vast and so grand.

Beijing and Shanghai with millions who stand.

Let's walk the Great Wall, won't you take my hand?

Where in the world will we go today?

Mexico, Mexico, what do you say?

Mexico, Mexico, so warm and so fun!

From the mountains of Monterrey to the Puerto
   Vallarta sun.
Visit Tulum, Chichen-Itza, and the city of Guaymas
   too.
See the art of their ancestors as you walk on through.

Where in the world will we go today?

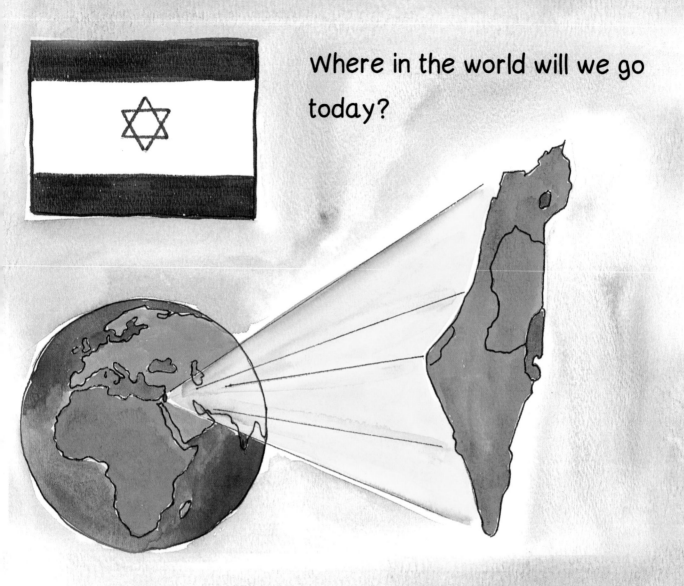

Israel, Israel, what do you say?

From Jerusalem to Tel Aviv, it is an ancient home.

Centuries of testaments, sharing what they know.
Walking trails that map the roads with miles and miles
   to see,
Think of all who journeyed there and who they may be!

Where in the world will we go today?

Australia, Australia, what do you say?

Australia is a continent too. It's a country and a continent too?

Indeed, it is absolutely true!

Travel through Sydney; It's the capital city.

Go swimming or snorkel the Great Barrier Reef,

And see fish and sharks that may cause you to shriek!

Kookaburras and kangaroos are a must see, for sure;

They live in the bush land, away from the shore.

Where in the world will we go today?

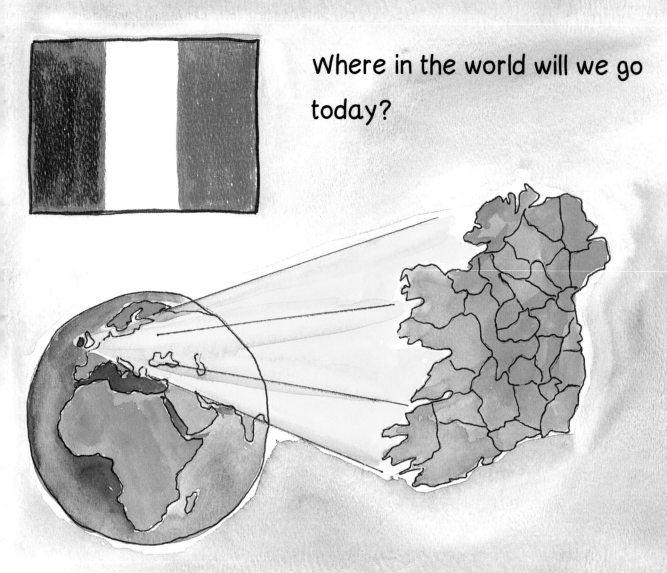

Ireland, Ireland, what do you say?
Ireland, Ireland, let's fly there today!
Go visit the Cliffs of Moher and Galway Bay.

Dublin is so fresh and so green,

With music, history, and air so clean!

In every part, the beauty amazes.

This country is one of my favorite places!

Where in the world will we go today?

Greece, Greece, what do you say?
Greece, Greece, it's one of a kind,
Old as the earth, the beginnings of mankind.

Go see for yourself how the Parthenon towered,

The city of Athens and all its great power.

The sights are unmatched, the
   monuments—breathtaking.

Greece is a place that is simply amazing!

Where in the world will we go today?

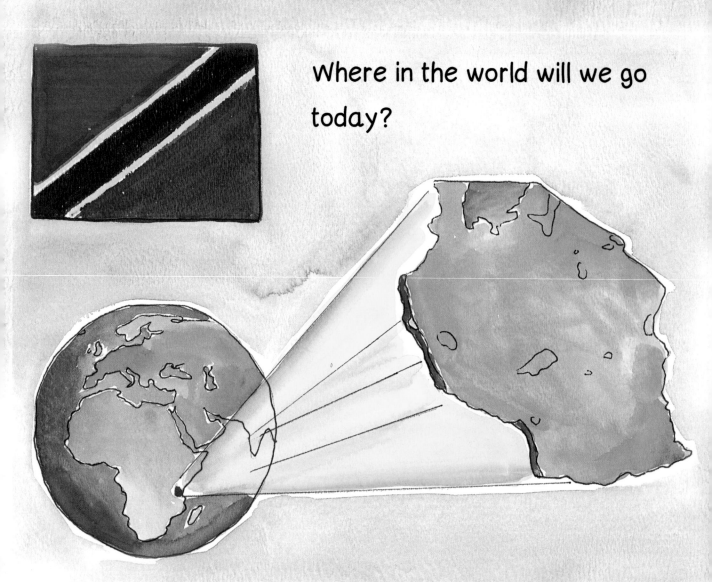

Tanzania, Tanzania, what do you say?
Tanzania, Tanzania, it's quite far away.

Tanzania is a country in Africa, with Mt. Kilimanjaro
  nestled there,
The highest mountain in a four hundred—mile square!
What else can we find when we visit Tanzania?
The waters of Lake Victoria so blue and bright,
With the moon shining down on the Serengeti at night.
The lions protect and watch their pack,
And the elephants graze on a yummy snack!

23

Where in the world will we go today?

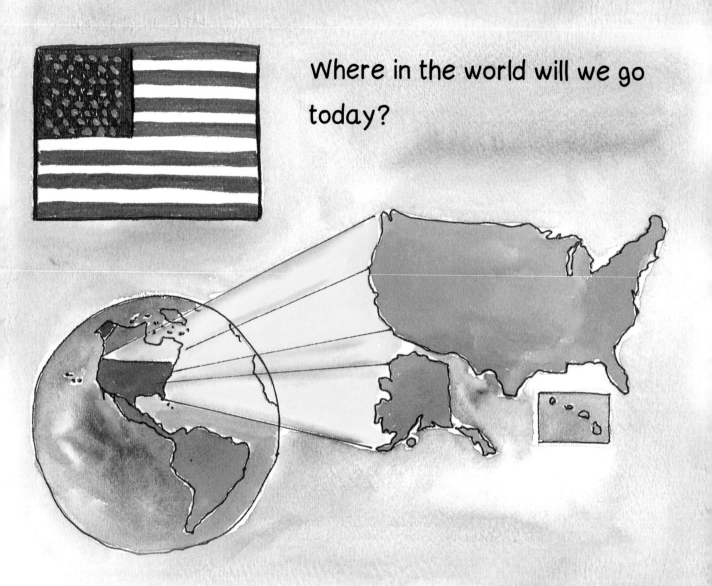

How about the good ol' U-S-of-A?

America, America, what do you say?

America is our chosen home.

There are millions who come and we continue to grow.

Our liberty, freedom, and all of our strength stem from
    the people who started this place!

With fifty plus states that are all so unique,

Wouldn't you like to know more about your own home
    state's treats?

Look at the map and tell me true . . . Point to the state
    that's home to you!

With that, my dear, we must say good-bye.
I hope you enjoyed our adventurous rhyme!

Where in the world will we go today?

This is our chant!

Anywhere! Everywhere!

There's nowhere we can't!